# FREEDOM

*Your Birthright as a Believer*

# FREEDOM

*Your Birthright as a Believer*

**ROBERT MORRIS**

# FREEDOM IS YOUR BIRTHRIGHT

One of the most beautiful pictures of Christ in the Bible is that of a Shepherd. Jesus describes Himself in John 10 as the *good shepherd*. *The good shepherd gives His life for the sheep* (verse 11). Jesus laid down His life so that we, His sheep, could have life through Him. He did not try to protect Himself; instead, He shed His blood out of love for us.

As our Shepherd, He wants to lead us to green pastures and still waters to restore our souls. He protects us from our enemies and desires to flood our lives with goodness and blessings. But there are others who also attempt to tend His flock. Jesus refers to them as thieves, robbers and hirelings (John 10:1–13). These have no concern for our well-being. Thieves and robbers come to steal, kill and destroy, and hirelings do nothing to protect us in the face of danger.

Life is wrought with dangerous paths, people and possibilities. Only in following the good Shepherd, listening to and heeding His voice, can we steer clear of the pitfalls and dangers. Most of us have lost sight of this Shepherd. The thieves, robbers and hirelings have taken over our care and have led us straight into the clutches of bondage.

What ever happened to the abundance Jesus came to give us? We have traded it in, whether knowingly or unknowingly, for addictions, fear, insecurities, bitterness and sinful indulgence. The enemy has convinced us we will find peace, joy and meaning in these things, and we have bought his lie. What is this "abundance" we are missing out on? Could the freedom found in Christ, our Shepherd, be better than the bondage our enemy, the thieves and robbers, have led us into?

Yes, it is! I say that from experience. If you are living in bondage, trust me, you want out. Life free from the shackles of the enemy is heaven on earth. Liberation from your chains is not as difficult as you might think. On the pages that follow, I walk you through how the enemy enslaves us and reveal the glorious truth of how Jesus can deliver us.

As you read, I pray God will restore your hope for an abundant life as you finally discover and walk in the freedom He created you to enjoy in this lifetime.

# CHAPTER ONE

# THE BULLY OF BONDAGE

I was a skinny kid, and though my body was small, my mouth was big. You can imagine that I found myself in some bad situations with that combination. It didn't take me long to realize that I was an easy target for bullies. My dad told me that if I stood up to a bully, he would back down. Well, my dad was wrong. Standing up to the tough guys didn't work out for me so well.

I developed my own strategy for survival: if you can't beat the big guys, join them. I decided to befriend the toughest kid in school—Gerald Gibson. Gerald and I became best friends. Whatever he needed or wanted, I was right there to oblige, and with Gerald by my side, the bullies didn't mess with me. They used to warn me that someday they'd find me without Gerald, and I would be toast. Luckily, that never happened.

My relationship with Gerald reminded me a lot of

Richie Cunningham and Arthur Fonzarelli. A recurring theme on *Happy Days* was that a bully would threaten Richie (for any variety of reasons), but Fonzie always showed up just in time to save him. As hard as it is to admit I was a goofy Richie Cunningham as a kid, I did make it through school okay because I had a Fonzie watching my back.

Bullies are not just a threat to scrawny kids on the playground. There is one bully who sets his sights on anyone and everyone, no matter their age or size, no matter how much money they have, where they live or who they know. This bully lives in the spiritual realm and will do anything, *anything* to terrorize us into bondage. If we give in to him, he will render us completely ineffective and unhappy.

Satan is the bully, and intimidation is his tactic to hold us back from all that God destined for us to have in Christ. His most effective weapon against God's people throughout history has always been deception. He is a really good liar! The first lie he ever pulled off was a doozie. Back in the Garden, Adam and Eve were created to carry the image and likeness of God without flaw. No one on earth was more like God than Adam and Eve were. But the devil came along and told Eve that by eating the fruit, she could be *like* God. She was already *like* God! Yet he convinced her to take the fruit.

Deception is exactly what Satan does. He comes to believers and tells us that if we will depart from God, we can have something God has already provided. To a married

Christian man, he might say that leaving his wife for that lady at work will give him fulfillment and joy. However, that man already has access to limitless joy in Christ. To a teenage girl, he might say that giving in to the pressure her boyfriend is putting on her to have sex will make him love and accept her more. When in Christ, she is completely accepted and unconditionally loved; she doesn't need her boyfriend to make her feel that way. Satan is a big fat liar, but we fall for his schemes all the time!

Where do we fall when we believe his lies? Right into the trap of bondage. No Christian should succumb to bondage. There is no reason one of God's children ever has to settle for that kind of life. It happens because the bully takes advantage of us in our moments of weakness to burden us with sin, problems or issues we can't get out of. At least we think we can't get out of them.

There is hope. You may feel like the scrawny kid on the playground who takes a beating day after day, but in the spirit realm, Jesus is your Fonzie. He is the toughest, coolest guy that no bully can beat, and He is on your side. Once Jesus lives in your heart, you have constant, go-to protection against all of the devil's lies and tricks. Jesus is with you every minute of every day and night, so you never have to settle for bondage.

This book is about learning to live in the deliverance Jesus died to give you. You don't have to wait for heaven to finally be free from those things that plague you and hold you back. Too many churches out there preach that Jesus came to save you from hell, but they don't tell you He can be just as powerful in your life today. He is the Fonz! Nothing is too hard for Him to overcome in your life.

Would you like to be finally free from that addiction, that chronic health problem, that fear, that anger, that sin? You can break through the bondage that is oppressing and suffocating the life out of you. God didn't send Jesus just to take us to heaven; He did it so even on earth we can get a taste of heaven. Life liberated from the oppression of the enemy and free to fully know and enjoy God is the eternal life Jesus died to give us.

It's time we stop giving in to the bully of bondage and start finding victory in Jesus.

## DON'T BELIEVE THE LIE

I once gave an impromptu quiz to the staff at my church. As I passed different staff members in the hall or had brief conversations with them, I asked what John 8:32 says. John 8:32 is a very well known verse in ministry circles, so all of them had an answer right away: *You shall know the truth and the truth shall make you free.* Every one of them said the same thing, but every one of them was wrong.

That night, as Debbie and I were going to bed, I extended the question to her. Maybe she could get it right.

"Debbie," I said, "what does John 8:32 say?"

Her answer was different from anyone else's that day. "Robert," she sounded exasperated, "it's way too late to be asking me that question."

I hope it's not too late to ask you the question. What John 8:32 has to say is vital for every Christian who needs a breakthrough in freedom. Do you know what it says? I will even make this an open book quiz. *And you shall know the truth, and the truth shall make you free*. The key word I want you to see here is the first word of the verse: *And ...*

When I failed all my co-ministers on the John 8:32 quiz, it was because they all left off the "and." This may sound like I am splitting hairs here, but I am making a very important distinction. The word "and" connects it to the previous verse, and that previous verse puts John 8:32 into an eye-opening context. Let's read the entire passage together: *Then Jesus said to those Jews who believed Him, "If you abide in My word, you are My disciples indeed. And you shall know the truth, and the truth shall make you free"* (John 8:31–32).

Who was Jesus talking to here? *... to those Jews who believed Him.* And what is the mark of being Jesus' disciple? *... abide in My word ...* So when Jesus explained that the truth sets people free, He was talking to believers. *And you shall know the truth, and the truth shall make you free* was a promise to believers.

As a believer, you need to know something: it is entirely

possible for a Christian to be in bondage. Somewhere along the way, a lie infiltrated the church and convinced us that if we are really Christians, we cannot ever live in bondage again. But here, in John 8, Jesus offers freedom to believers, which means, even Christians can be in bondage.

How does that happen? If Jesus' death conquered Satan, how do we, His followers, become enslaved again? Jesus answers that a couple of verses later: *Most assuredly, I say to you, whoever commits sin is a slave of sin* (John 8:34). It's that simple. Sin enslaves us in bondage.

Since every one of us sins, is this saying every one of us is in bondage? Not exactly. The Greek word here for "commits sin" actually refers to "prolonged" or "continuing sin." What Jesus is saying to these Jewish believers and to us today is that whoever participates in continuing sin without coming to Him in repentance, without even an effort to turn away from it, is in bondage.

Because believers still sin after they put their faith in Christ, we are all still in danger of bondage. Being a Christian doesn't make you immune to the threat of oppression. Many Christians think their problems aren't a result of bondage, so they beat themselves up over their struggles and never learn to live in the victory Christ made available to them.

How do you know if you are in bondage? The answer is found in one word—chronic. Chronic sins, behaviors or problems point directly to bondage. If you have chronic financial issues, there is an area of spiritual bondage behind it all. If you have chronic health issues, meaning you are sick over and over again, if your whole body is plagued with illness, there could be a spirit of bondage holding you back from physical freedom. If you have chronic relational issues, not just with one person but in all areas of your life, somehow Satan has enslaved you. If you have a sin issue, something that you want to stop doing, but can't no matter how hard you try, you are in bondage.

Bondage is real. Satan and his demons are experts at binding and gagging the followers of Jesus and then convincing us we are not in bondage at all. The spiritual realm is real, and the powers of darkness play no games. They are after you and will do whatever it takes to keep you tied down so you cannot operate in the fullness God destined for you.

I looked up the words "demon(s)" and "demon-possessed" in the Bible and discovered both the Old Testament and New Testament referred to them hundreds of times. Demons didn't just show up when Jesus walked the earth, and they didn't go away as soon as He ascended back into heaven. They've been around since the fall of mankind, and they are still alive and active today. You don't have to go to Africa or the jungles of South America to find them. They are in America too. In Africa, the people they hold in bondage may look like witchdoctors, but in America, they wear suits and drive minivans.

Demons are among us, and they are still deceiving us today. They are still seizing every opportunity to turn difficulty in our lives into bondage. We have to confront them and deal with them if we ever really want to be free from their grasp. We can't go on pretending in the church that demons are imaginary or are not a problem for us.

I have a friend who got saved when he was a hippie and decided to become a missionary. To prepare for missions, he went to a school in Costa Rica with believers from various backgrounds and churches. He didn't grow up in the church and wasn't really up on different denominations and beliefs, so he spoke freely and openly to other students there about demons and the spiritual warfare he had encountered.

One day, he was talking to a guy about demons, and the guy explained that his church didn't cast out demons. "Oh," responded my friend perplexed. "You don't cast demons out of people in your church? Hmmm, what do you do? Just leave 'em in there?"

Since he had become a Christian, my friend had seen the reality of the spiritual realm. It never occurred to him that there were some believers out there who were oblivious to it. It didn't make sense to him why churches weren't exercising Jesus' authority over Satan and casting out demons.

The moment we become Christians, the Holy Spirit

baptizes us into the Body of Christ and marks us for heaven. From that point on, we should seek out His constant and continued filling. The way we are continually filled with the Spirit is by yielding to His influence. As we hand over areas of our lives to Him, He controls more and more of us. The same is true of evil spirits. The more we yield to their influence in our lives, the more control they take. The more control they have, the harder it is for us to break free from their grip.

Satan and his demons operate best in darkness. They know that as long as they can convince you that you are not in bondage, they have control of you. Don't buy their lie. Ask God to reveal to you those areas of chronic behavior that are restricting you from walking in freedom and enjoying the blessings Jesus died to give you. Once you see those areas of bondage, admit it. Get it out into the light. Once it is out there, the power of darkness is defeated and you are on your way to freedom.

Whatever it is—immorality, anger, drugs, addiction, sickness, debt—Jesus can set you free. His truth has the power to set any believer free. Demons only have as much power over us as we give them. Shine the light on their schemes and turn to Jesus to rescue you from their grip.

## BAD NEWS ABOUT BONDAGE

I know I make all this sound easy, this getting free from bondage. To be completely honest with you, it isn't all easy. There is one part of finding freedom that is really, really hard. It is actually the very first step of the process: fessin' up. Admitting you are in bondage is the most difficult part of getting free from bondage.

When Jesus was talking to the Jewish believers back in John 8, telling them the truth was enough to set them free, they responded with resistance and pride. They said, *We are Abraham's descendants, and have never been in bondage to anyone. How can You say, "You will be made free?"* (John 8:33).

If we slow down to read this passage, it is actually really funny. Listen to what these Jews are saying to Jesus here: "What are you talking about Jesus? You don't need to set *us* free. We are Abraham's descendants and have *never* been in *bondage* to *anyone!*" Have you ever read the Bible or just seen the movie? They had been in bondage to everyone— Egypt, Chaldea, Babylon, Greece and Assyria. The very Jews who made the claim that they had *never* been in bondage to *anyone* were at that very moment in bondage to *Rome!*

As much as this makes us chuckle, we are no better. Christians today are plagued with hate, unforgiveness, insecurity, addiction. You name it, we struggle with it, yet we still say, "I'm a Christian. I couldn't be in bondage." Oh yes you are! Wherever there is prolonged or continued sin, there is bondage.

The reason bondage is hard for us to admit is because it reveals what is going on inside of us. Man is extremely sensitive to internal, heart issues. Our pride forces us to deny there is anything wrong with us on the inside. This pride problem doesn't go away when we become Christians, either. In fact, I think it gets worse. We take on the expectation that Christians are supposed to have achieved some higher level of morality and that we should not struggle with anything ... so we lie. Even though we are dying on the inside, we smile and say nothing is wrong.

In church, you may feel like the only unholy one who has bad thoughts or does bad things. You may look around at the "spiritual" people who fill the pews and think they have it all together while you are falling apart. "Maybe," the devil whispers in your ear, "you should stop coming to this church before you ruin the whole thing."

Let me give you just a tidbit of truth containing the power to set you free from a lie that has held you down for years: no matter how pretty everyone looks at church, they've all got problems just like you. You are not the only unholy one. Apart from the grace of Jesus, we are all unholy.

God wants you to break free from the idea that you have to appear perfect to fit into His family. He wants you to admit what is really going on in your heart so He can set you free. As long as you hide behind fear or shame, whatever chronic problem you have will hold you in bondage.

I know it is hard to fess up, but I promise you, it is worth it. Go to the Lord or a trusted friend or family member and just admit you are in bondage.

The first step is the hardest, but after you get the admitting part down, the burden transfers from you to Jesus.

## GOOD NEWS ABOUT BONDAGE

After working through the hurdles of step one—putting away your pride and lowering the mask of pretense—step two has some great news for us. It is the easy part. The actual process of being set free can only be done by Jesus, so unlike step one, this step does not depend on you. The even better news is that Jesus has already done the hard work of setting you free. On the cross, He defeated the devil once and for all!

The devil and his demons might scare us, but Jesus is neither impressed, nor intimidated by them. Back when Jesus walked the earth, He sent 70 of His disciples equipped with His power to preach His kingdom, heal the sick and cast out demons. When they returned, this was their report:

> *17 Then the seventy returned with joy, saying, "Lord, even the demons are subject to us in Your name." 18 And He said to them, "I saw Satan fall like lightning from heaven. 19 Behold, I give you the authority to trample on serpents and scorpions, and over all the power of*

*the enemy, and nothing shall by any means hurt you.*
*²⁰ Nevertheless do not rejoice in this, that the spirits are*
*subject to you, but rather rejoice because your names*
*are written in heaven"* (Luke 10:17–20).

These 70 came back astounded at how the demons trembled at just the sound of Jesus' name. When they told Jesus about it His response to them was not, "Really?! The demons were afraid of *Me*? How cool!" Nope. In essence, what Jesus said was, "Guys, I'm not impressed that those demons obeyed you when you used My name. They've been obeying me for thousands of years. I created them, and I watched them fall from heaven. Even though they rebelled against God, they still have to do what I say."

The only thing Jesus has to do to get a demon out of your life is say, "Boo!" He has had that authority for a long time. He is unimpressed with Satan and his demons, and He expects us to be unimpressed as well. What He wants us to get excited and worked up over is that we are now on our way to heaven instead of hell.

Whatever demon is holding you captive, Jesus isn't scared. He has complete authority to cast that demon aside and set you free. One of my favorite times Jesus cast out a demon is recorded in Mark 9:

*¹⁷ Then one of the crowd answered and said, "Teacher,*

*I brought You my son, who has a mute spirit. ¹⁸ And wherever it seizes him, it throws him down; he foams at the mouth, gnashes his teeth, and becomes rigid. So I spoke to Your disciples, that they should cast it out, but they could not." ¹⁹ He answered him and said, "O faithless generation, how long shall I be with you? How long shall I bear with you? Bring him to Me." ²⁰ Then they brought him to Him. And when he saw Him, immediately the spirit convulsed him, and he fell on the ground and wallowed, foaming at the mouth. ²¹ So He asked his father, "How long has this been happening to him?" And he said, "From childhood. ²² And often he has thrown him both into the fire and into the water to destroy him. But if You can do anything, have compassion on us and help us." ²³ Jesus said to him, "If you can believe, all things are possible to him who believes." ²⁴ Immediately the father of the child cried out and said with tears, "Lord, I believe; help my unbelief!" ²⁵ When Jesus saw that the people came running together, He rebuked the unclean spirit, saying to it, "Deaf and dumb spirit, I command you, come out of him and enter him no more!" ²⁶ Then the spirit cried out, convulsed him greatly, and came out of him. And he became as one dead, so that many said, "He is dead." ²⁷ But Jesus took him by the hand and lifted him up, and he arose* (Mark 9:17–27).

Again, if we slow down to read this and picture in our minds what is going on, it is almost funny. Jesus had just come down from being on top of a mountain where He talked with Moses, Elijah and His Father. While He had been up there reveling in the absolute wonder of the supernatural, His disciples had been back in town wrestling with a demon-possessed kid, unable to help him at all. When the father approached Him, Jesus looked at His guys and said, "What am I going to do with you? This is so easy! Step aside. I'll take care of it."

The boy got close to Jesus and started flopping around on the ground and foaming at the mouth. Just imagine it. There had to be quite a crowd gathering to watch this spectacle, gawking while guarding themselves from potential harm. Then there was Jesus. Notice He didn't freak out and jump on the boy to get control of the situation. I personally think He was leaning up against a fence post, munching on an apple when He casually looked at the dad and asked, "Hmm, how long's he been like this?" Just as calm as He could be.

In desperation, the man says to Jesus, ... *if You* can do anything ... help us.

"*If I* ... " Jesus said. "If *I* ... no, no, no. The question here is not if *I* am able. Fella, you got it backward. *I* am able to do anything. The point is, *if you* can believe, then I will take care of it."

There is no bondage Jesus cannot take care of. A boy possessed by such evil demons that they regularly tried to kill him was an easy task for Jesus. Whatever you are struggling with is no match for Jesus' power and authority.

Bondage is a bully because some of you out there actually believe you can never change or be free. The demons have you convinced addiction, pain, sin, sickness or whatever is your lot in life, but Jesus is saying to you, "Not *if I* can set you free, but *if you* can believe." Do you believe? Even a small amount of faith is enough. The father in this story admitted, *Lord, I believe; help my unbelief!* Maybe you should make that your prayer today. Go to Jesus with the bondage that is holding your head under water, throwing you into the fire and trying to destroy you. Then with all the faith you can muster, ask Him to increase your belief and to help you. He can do it. He will do it.

Jesus can set you free from bondage ... that is good news.

## MAKE THAT FIRST STEP

Jesus told us that wherever there is sin, there is bondage. In every chronic problem area, there is a sin issue at its root. This is why admission and confession are so important. Bondage is a heart issue that has to be dealt with on a heart level. You have to go deep and confess the sin that has put you in bondage. Jesus can set you free because He has already conquered your sin.

James 5:16 says, *Confess your trespasses to one another, and pray for one another, that you may be healed. The effective, fervent prayer of a righteous man avails much.* The first step is confessing your sin, but not just to God. We don't repent by only talking to God quietly in our minds. No, James tells us the healing comes from confessing to one another.

Again, Satan works in darkness, and his grip on you depends upon you keeping the light off of what is going on. Admitting to one of your brothers or sisters in Christ that you are struggling in bondage shines a spotlight on the prince of darkness, and he will cower under the exposure. Light doesn't only penetrate darkness; it completely expels darkness.

If you want to break the power the devil has over your life, speak up about what is going on. Ninety percent of the devil's power will be lost as soon as you do that. As your fellow believers pray for you and have faith with you that Christ can overcome, you will experience healing and breakthrough you never knew were possible.

As a pastor, I plead with people to take part in our small groups. Every week, I encourage those who sit on the fringe of our community to dive deeply into relationships with other believers. I fully believe that breakthrough and healing happen in these small groups. As you open up to one another, intimacy, trust and accountability are fostered.

Don't just be a weekend Christian. Get involved in relationships with other believers wherever possible so they can pray for you and walk with you toward your healing and deliverance. Jesus already has done His part. Receiving His help is the easy part. You just have to take that difficult first step of opening up, shedding light in the darkness, so you can be liberated by the power of Jesus.

# CHAPTER TWO

# GATEWAYS TO BONDAGE

Elevating to a new level in this area of freedom is about more than breaking free from something ... it is about being released to something. If God's only concern were to rescue you from the grip of the devil, He would go about it a lot differently. The breakthrough He wants to give you is to a life far greater than you knew possible. He has a destiny, a purpose He designed especially for you to live out. Bondage makes it impossible, but breaking free from bondage opens doors to a new, abundant and rewarding life.

Jesus didn't die just so you could stop drinking too much beer or get over an eating disorder. That is such a small part of the picture. Jesus suffered, bled and died not just so you could go to heaven, but so you could become like Him even on this earth.

Right now, if God were to open your eyes to all He has in store for you, if you could in an instant see the full potential and destiny of your life, you just might pass out. In His heart, God has a vision for your life that is so dynamic. The bondage you are settling for is devastating. If only you could peek into His mind, into His intentions, I believe you would lay down whatever sin issues you are flirting with and instead embrace what He has for you.

That is why this book on freedom is so important for you. The implications of elevating to a new level of freedom in your life can affect your family, your health, your finances, your future, your ministry ... every part of your life. Remaining content with the bondage you have grown accustomed to living with is settling for so much less than you were created to have and do.

Where have you allowed the devil to gain a foothold in your life? Where has sin taken you captive? What chronic problems have you spiraling down into a cycle of defeat?

For every area of bondage you remain in, the enemy gains ground in your life. Every time you open the door to him, you welcome him in to wreak his havoc. Sometimes we don't even realize it is happening, but nonetheless, the devil comes in and stakes his claim, binding us in such confining restraints that our potential is either lost or put on indefinite hold.

Even when you get free from bondage, don't think Satan will leave you alone. He is determined to keep you down. He has schemes that have worked for millennia, and he won't hesitate to use them on you. Jesus told us, *Most assuredly, I say to you, he who does not enter the sheepfold by the door, but climbs up some other way, the same is a thief and a robber* (John 10:1). Satan is not our shepherd, so he cannot get to us the way our Shepherd does. He has to come in *some other way.*

In this chapter, I want to highlight five *other ways* Satan sneaks into the sheepfold to lead us into bondage. Once he is in, he will accomplish his purposes which Jesus goes on to tell us are *to steal, and to kill, and to destroy* (John 10:10). Until he has stolen from you, killed you and destroyed you, he will not leave you alone. By becoming aware of the gateways he is using to get into your sheepfold, you can head him off before he leads you astray into any more bondage.

## BOUND FROM BIRTH

The first way Satan gets into our lives almost seems unfair because he came at you long before you could ever have known he was dangerous. I've already told you that sin leads to bondage, but there are certain sins you are particularly predisposed to. When you were born, you already had an inclination toward them. The devil exploits these sins from your earliest childhood days.

Exodus 20:5 says, *For I, the Lord your God, am a jealous God, visiting the iniquity of the fathers upon the children to the third and fourth generations ...* You may be struggling with sin or the consequences of sin that you never invited into your life. Your parents, grandparents, even your great-great grandparents may have gotten involved in sin, and today you are paying the consequences. If you do the math, you will see that you carry the sin baggage of the 30 people who make up your most recent family tree.

Like I said, it doesn't seem fair, but that is the depth of devastation sin causes. In whatever area you die in bondage to sin, you pass a predisposition toward that sin to your descendents as well. Since that is true, the weight of the discussion about chronic sin in our lives just got heavier. The consequences will carry on after you for generations.

Again, I know it sounds completely unfair. Most of us don't struggle with the concept that some illnesses are genetic. Heart disease or allergies might be passed from mother to daughter, and we accept this as a fact of life. In the same way, sin passes from parent to child. Addiction, racism, depression, alcoholism, etc. can take hold in a family line and haunt generation after generation.

This phenomenon is known as a generational curse. The curse upon us is the tendency in our hearts toward certain sins our fathers were guilty of. The curse is not the sin itself, but the bent toward that sin. That bent or tendency is known in the Bible as "iniquity" whereas acting on the tendency is called "sin." For example, lust is the iniquity and adultery is the sin. Hate is the iniquity and murder is the sin. The iniquity is the inner movement, the heart condition, while the sin is the outworking of the iniquity. I like to say it this way:

- Iniquity is the inward motivation.
- Sin is the outward movement.
- Iniquity is the attitude.
- Sin is the action.
- Iniquity is the heart.
- Sin is the hand.
- It's those inner bondages that are passed down from generation to generation.

*6 " ... I will not keep silence, but will repay—Even repay into their bosom—7 Your iniquities and the iniquities of your fathers together," Says the Lord ...* (Isaiah 65:6–7).

*40 But if they confess their iniquity and the iniquity of their fathers, with their unfaithfulness in which they were unfaithful to Me, and that they also have walked contrary to Me, 41 and that I also have walked contrary to them and have brought them into the land of their enemies; if their uncircumcised hearts are humbled, and they accept their guilt—42 then I will remember My covenant with Jacob, and My covenant with Isaac and My covenant with Abraham I will remember; I will remember the land* (Leviticus 26:40–42).

*We acknowledge, O LORD, our wickedness And the iniquity of our fathers, For we have sinned against You* (Jeremiah 14:20).

God holds us responsible for the iniquities of our fathers. They were passed down to us, and unless we allow God to break the cycle, we will repeat their sins and pass them down to our children, grandchildren, great-grandchildren and great-great grandchildren.

You have no idea how much filth your ancestors got themselves into. Quite frankly, you were born lugging so much baggage, and you don't even know what is in the suitcases! Those generational curses are one of the first ways the devil comes at you. He knows what your parents did. He knows the bondage your grandparents were in. He even remembers your great-great grandparents. The devil knows whatever they struggled with will be your weak areas, so he comes at you there first.

Somewhere along the line of generational curses, somebody has to put his foot down. Israel confessed the iniquities of their fathers so God would look on them with fresh grace and mercy. In repenting of the sins their ancestors had committed, they put a stop to the continuance of that curse.

Today is the day generational curses can end in your family. You can make a choice for your family that will affect generations to come. After God said He visits the iniquity of

the fathers upon the children to the third and fourth generation, He also said He shows *mercy to thousands, to those
who love Me and keep My commandments* (Exodus 20:6).
Your choice to love God and follow His ways has more far-
reaching consequences than your sin has.

At the end of this chapter, I will walk you through a
prayer that will help you put an end to the generational
curses that have you in bondage today. More than likely, it
will be just the beginning of the process of the Holy Spirit
showing you which bondage is a result of the iniquity
passed down to you. As you discover tendencies toward
sin that keep you shackled to a lifestyle of disobedience
toward God, you can confess your actions as well as your
ancestors' so the curse can be broken.

This is huge for you and your children. Being set free
from generational bondage is a work only God can do, and
you can be sure, He wants to do it for you and the generations that will come behind you.

## BOUND IN UNFORGIVENESS

We've all heard it: *do not let the sun go down on your wrath*
(Ephesians 4:26). It's such a common command to most of
us, but why is it so hard? You have a fight with your spouse
just after dinner and all the Bible asks you to do is resolve
the issue before you go to bed, but you don't. That guy
at work took credit for an idea you had and all the Bible

tells you to do is to talk to him and forgive him before the end of day, but you don't. What is holding us back? I'll tell you—that deep-seated craving for justice. We want that person who offended us to repent, and we will hang on to our anger until he does.

Let me tell you something. Your anger is not hurting him as much as it's hurting you. Being mad at someone actually causes him little, if any, harm, but what it does inside of you ... well, it's bad. Ephesians 4 goes on to say that unresolved anger gives the devil an entry point into your life. As we've seen in other areas, once the enemy finds a way into your sheepfold, he will bully you into the corner of bondage and hold you prisoner.

The writer of Hebrews brings up an interesting consequence of anger: *Pursue peace with all people ... lest any root of bitterness springing up cause trouble, and by this many become defiled ...* (Hebrews 12:14–15). The word for "defiled" here means sexual sin. Many people have a propensity toward sexual immorality because they let the sun set on their anger. It may be a 20-year-old grievance against a family member or friend, but they continue to carry around unforgiveness and bitterness, holding them in a bondage that leads them to sexual immorality.

I'm not saying that everyone who sleeps around does so because deep down they are mad at someone, but I am saying that bitterness could be the cause, as could a generational curse. It is important to get to the source of our sin issues so we can uproot the problem. Unless the root of sin is destroyed, it will continue to sprout up into issues that cause us and those around us even more pain.

God is our ultimate example of forgiveness. If you don't know how to let go of the offense someone committed against you, look back at all God has forgiven you of. In fact, meditation on God's grace toward you might be just the kick in the pants you need to finally forgive and be free from the bondage of bitterness.

Jesus told us a story of the consequences of withholding the forgiveness He has given us:

> *23 Therefore the kingdom of heaven is like a certain king who wanted to settle accounts with his servants. 24 And when he had begun to settle accounts, one was brought to him who owed him ten thousand talents. 25 But as he was not able to pay, his master commanded that he be sold, with his wife and children and all that he had, and that payment be made. 26 The servant therefore fell down before him, saying, "Master, have patience with me, and I will pay you all." 27 Then the master of that servant was moved with compassion, released him, and forgave him the debt.*

> *28 But that servant went out and found one of his fellow*

*servants who owed him a hundred denarii; and he laid hands on him and took him by the throat, saying, "Pay me what you owe!"29 So his fellow servant fell down at his feet and begged him, saying, "Have patience with me, and I will pay you all." 30 And he would not, but went and threw him into prison till he should pay the debt. 31 So when his fellow servants saw what had been done, they were very grieved, and came and told their master all that had been done. 32 Then his master, after he had called him, said to him, "You wicked servant! I forgave you all that debt because you begged me. 33 Should you not also have had compassion on your fellow servant, just as I had pity on you?" 34 And his master was angry, and delivered him to the torturers until he should pay all that was due to him.*

*35 So My heavenly Father also will do to you if each of you, from his heart, does not forgive his brother his trespasses"* (Matthew 18:23–35).

The first servant went before the king owing what equates to $50 million in today's economy. Having been pardoned from such tremendous debt, rescued from a lifetime of slavery for him and his family, the servant then turned around and imprisoned one who could not repay a loan of only $44.

This story seems so extreme that it is impossible to

miss Jesus' point. God has forgiven us more than we could ever imagine to repay in a lifetime, yet we refuse to extend that same forgiveness to others. What strikes me about this passage is what the master did to the first servant when He found out how uncompassionate he had been toward his fellow servant: He delivered him over to the torturers. In the story, such a punishment makes complete sense, but when we apply the parable to our situation and the bitterness we bear toward others, do we think we deserve torture?

Jesus said God will do the same to us when we do not forgive others of their trespasses. It is not Satan who delivers you to the torturers, but God Himself. Who are the torturers? Demon spirits. When we refuse to forgive others, God hands us over to the very bondage He set us free from.

Do I sound like I'm contradicting myself? On one page I say God wants you to be free from bondage, and on the next page I tell you He delivers you over to that same bondage. Well, God does not contradict Himself with His words or His actions. He loves you, and everything He does is for your good. The reason He delivers us over to bondage when we don't forgive is because He loves us.

Let me explain what I mean. God imagines for you the greatest possible destiny—to be close to Him. Intimate relationship with Him is the greatest dream of His heart for all of His children. He created us with a longing only He can fill, and He wants us to come to Him to fill that longing. Unforgiveness is about as far from His character as you can get. When you embrace unforgiveness, you are running from His presence. The more you wrap yourself in bitterness and anger, the farther from Him you drift.

The most merciful thing God can do for you in that situation is to turn you over to the torturers. If you do not feel the consequences of distancing yourself from God, you will never want to return to Him. If you continue down that road without the loving hand of God plaguing it with so much pain that you want to turn back, the only end you will find is more sin, pain, bondage and destruction. Turning us over to the torturers is the Father's way of helping us see the foolishness of our anger so we can forgive and be restored to a right relationship with Him once again.

Unforgiveness is like drinking poison in hope that it will kill the person who hurt you. It's never going to happen. The poison will only kill you. The only antidote to the poison you've been swallowing is forgiveness. Forgiveness will set you free.

I've counseled some people who held the misconception that forgiving someone is condoning what the person did. What you say with your forgiveness is, "I choose to offer you the same grace God gave to me. I know that He is the ultimate Judge and He will deal with your offense against me. But I will not be infected by the disease of bitterness."

Friends, every time you harbor unforgiveness in your

heart toward someone, it opens another gate to the devil, and you sink deeper into bondage. It is time to let go of the weight that is pulling you down. Don't let unforgiveness drown you. The torture you're experiencing is God calling you back to His presence. The way to close the gate on Satan and open the gate to your loving Shepherd is to forgive just as you have been forgiven.

## BOUND IN TRAUMA

Our enemy is shameless. He will do anything to entrap people in darkness. He will even attack children.

My friend Marcus who serves with me on staff at Gateway Church was only 11 years old when the devil took advantage of a traumatic situation in his life. He and his family arrived home from dinner to discover thieves robbing their house. Marcus was the first one through the door, so he was the first to see the burglars. In a moment, he went from being the most secure little boy to the most insecure. The place he had always thought to be the safest in the world had been violated.

At night, while the rest of his family lay sleeping peacefully in their beds, Marcus would lie awake, sweat dripping down his face, trembling with fear. He listened to every creak, every noise from the hallway with horror at the thought of intruders creeping closer and closer to his room. Marcus, at the young age of 11, was in bondage to fear.

When you bear witness to or experience a traumatic event, the devil is given a split-second opportunity of fear or pain, which he can use to gain entrance into your heart. He never misses this chance. He sinks his hooks in you, no matter how innocent or safe you might feel. No one is invulnerable to such an attack.

This type of bondage is the most heartbreaking to me. It isn't a result of prolonged sin. It wasn't passed down to you from those who sinned for generations. It happens simply because you experienced something outside of your control. You were at the wrong place at the wrong time, and Satan took the opportunity.

Jesus has such tenderness and love toward those who are in such bondage. *A bruised reed He will not break, And smoking flax He will not quench* (Matthew 12:20). He is gentle with bruised people, treating them with compassion. When you come to Him with the pain of trauma and the bondage it trapped you in, He will not scold you. Jesus only wants to heal you of your pain and set you free from the hold it still has on you.

So many people remain in the bondage of trauma because they are afraid to talk about it. They think people will think they are weird. After the trauma they've been through, the last thing they need is rejection, so they keep it all inside. They hold their wound, as the demons hold them in bondage.

I am convinced all fear is a fear of death. Someone might say he is afraid of heights, but he is actually afraid of falling to his death from something high. Or someone might say she is afraid of snakes, but actually she is afraid of one biting and killing her. We fear what we believe will kill us. The fear that trapped you in the moment of trauma was a fear of death, and the fear that convinces you to keep your bondage a secret is also a fear of death.

Hebrews 2:14–15 says, *[Jesus] Himself likewise shared in the same, that through death He might destroy him who had the power of death, that is, the devil, and release those who through fear of death were all their lifetime subject to bondage.* This is the incredible promise we cling to. Jesus already destroyed the one who holds the power of death. For Jesus' followers, there is no death, so there is no reason to fear.

It is natural to succumb to fear in the moment of trauma, but you have to recognize what Satan accomplishes in that moment as well. He traps us in fear and holds us prisoner there until we give that fear over to the one who has conquered death. For a believer, trauma does not have to be and should never be a lifetime area of bondage.

It was a cheap move on Satan's part to get you in bondage, and it was a costly victory on Jesus' part to set you free. Choose Jesus' freedom and break free from the enemy's hold on you.

## BOUND ON THE ENEMY'S GROUND

When I say the word "witch," you may get a mental picture of an old, ugly woman with a pointed hat and toothless grin bent over a steaming cauldron with her broomstick in her hand. Such an image is not reality; it is just a storybook version. Witchcraft and the occult are real communities and practices that openly promote Satan's kingdom of darkness.

I doubt anyone reading this book would deny that witchcraft and the occult are evil. Most of us are quick to agree that no Christian should be involved in them. Sadly, many believers have been or are involved without even realizing the danger.

While you may vow never to get involved in such dark practices, consider what 1 Samuel 15:23 says: *For rebellion is as the sin of witchcraft, And stubbornness is as iniquity and idolatry.* At its core, witchcraft is rebellion against God. No matter how much we all try to deny it, we've all rebelled against Him at one time or another. Stubbornly defying God's authority and rule on this earth and in our own lives is equated in this verse to witchcraft.

Of course, the outworking of witchcraft and the occult results in far more than rebellion or stubbornness. Those who lift themselves over God spiritually often partake in such activities as talking to the dead, divining the future by the stars or tarot cards and summoning the power of the evil one for evil purposes. These are seriously dangerous activities because they challenge God's ultimate power and attempt to give His glory to the devil.

Again, I don't think anyone reading this book is eager to glorify Satan, but unless you are aware of how crafty our enemy is at roping us into these activities, you may walk in blindly and find yourself captive to bondage on the very ground of the enemy. Friends, it is never safe even to dabble in the activity of the occult.

Deuteronomy 18:10–12 gives a stern warning to all of God's people:

> *[10] There shall not be found among you anyone who makes his son or his daughter pass through the fire, or one who practices witchcraft, or a soothsayer, or one who interprets omens, or a sorcerer, [11] or one who conjures spells, or a medium, or a spiritist, or one who calls up the dead. [12] For all who do these things are an abomination to the Lord, and because of these abominations the Lord your God drives them out from before you.*

Such strong language should not be taken lightly. In modern American society, the occult is alive and well, but it is often passed on to an unassuming public as harmless and interesting. Horoscopes hold a regular spot in the daily paper. Psychic hotlines are advertised on television. Ouija boards, "Dungeons & Dragons" and "Light as a Feather" are marketed as fun ways to entertain children.

Don't believe the hype. When you call that psychic, plan your day around your horoscope or allow your kids to play occultist games, you are walking into the middle of enemy territory unprotected. Be assured that the devil won't miss such a golden opportunity to enslave you.

I urge you, don't take the spiritual realm lightly. Jesus paid the ultimate price to defeat the very darkness we so often flirt with. Instead, we should stand by Jesus' side, renouncing Satan's kingdom, his schemes, his plots and his followers who exalt him as though he were equal to God. If you have dabbled in witchcraft or the occult before, confess it to God and to a friend and ask Jesus to deliver you from any stronghold it holds in your life.

## BOUND IN SIN

Up to this point, we've discussed ways the enemy gets into our lives. In each of the four ways I've mentioned, there has been an element of victimization involved, something Satan took advantage of in your life that you couldn't naturally avoid:

- You were born with curses passed down through the generations which give you a natural propensity toward sin. You can't control what family you are born into.

- People in your life have hurt and offended you. You were innocent.
- Because you were "at the wrong place at the wrong time," you were involved in a traumatic event. Satan took advantage.
- Unknowingly, you took part in things that were of the occult. The enemy pounced.

Again, Satan has no qualms about taking advantage of what life throws your way. In fact, he cunningly takes part in what he can to lead you down the wrong path. He will do whatever it takes to imprison you, torment you and destroy you.

In this last section, I want to talk about the path to bondage that is no one's fault but our own. We can't pass the buck here to anyone but the person we see in the mirror. The last gateway to bondage I want to discuss is sin, an invitation to the devil to lock us up and throw away the key.

Romans 6:16 says, *Do you not know that to whom you present yourselves slaves to obey, you are that one's slaves whom you obey, whether of sin leading to death, or of obedience leading to righteousness?* In this life, it is inevitable—you will be a slave to something. We all obey someone or something, which makes us all slaves. You do have a choice about whom you will swear your allegiance to. When you live in continuous, unrepentant sin, you present yourself a slave to that sin. Satan will make sure that your master, sin, only brings death into your life. On the other hand, you could choose to obey God instead. Submitting to God's ways in your life is the best kind of slavery because it ultimately leads to abundant life and the freedom of righteousness.

When you sin, you build a fort for the enemy to set up camp and wage war against your soul. Every time you give in, you fortify thought patterns, behaviors and habits, constructing a stronghold so high and impenetrable that escape seems hopeless. It took you years to build the fort and strongholds, and it will take time to disassemble them.

Jesus has already won the victory over your sin and the one who holds you captive to that sin. There is no question that in a moment's time, He can deliver you from the power the enemy has lorded over you. However, your deliverance will not be the end of your fight. You still have to demolish the habits and strongholds brick by brick, day by day, decision by decision.

Bad habits are hard to defeat, but I've learned a helpful tip in getting rid of them: get rid of the demons, and the habits will fall much easier. When the demons are hanging on, it is impossible to let go. You may suffer with an addiction you've tried over and over to quit but just can't. I promise you, once Jesus delivers you from the enemy's grip in that part of your life, saying no and denying yourself the indulgence of that addiction will come much easier. As my good friend, Pastor Jack Hayford says, "You can't disciple a demon!"

I want to conclude this chapter with a story about a demon-possessed man who encountered Jesus.

> *¹ Then they came to the other side of the sea, to the country of the Gadarenes. ² And when He had come out of the boat, immediately there met Him out of the tombs a man with an unclean spirit, ³ who had his dwelling among the tombs; and no one could bind him, not even with chains, ⁴ because he had often been bound with shackles and chains. And the chains had been pulled apart by him, and the shackles broken in pieces; neither could anyone tame him. ⁵ And always, night and day, he was in the mountains and in the tombs, crying out and cutting himself with stones.*

> *⁶ When he saw Jesus from afar, he ran and worshiped Him. ⁷ And he cried out with a loud voice and said, "What have I to do with You, Jesus, Son of the Most High God? I implore You by God that You do not torment me."*

> *⁸ For He said to him, "Come out of the man, unclean spirit!" ⁹ Then He asked him, "What is your name?"*

*And he answered, saying, "My name is Legion; for we
are many." ¹⁰ Also he begged Him earnestly that He
would not send them out of the country.*

*¹¹ Now a large herd of swine was feeding there near
the mountains. ¹² So all the demons begged Him, saying, "Send us to the swine, that we may enter them."
¹³ And at once Jesus gave them permission. Then the
unclean spirits went out and entered the swine (there
were about two thousand); and the herd ran violently
down the steep place into the sea, and drowned in the
sea* (Mark 5:1–13).

This guy was naked, living in a cemetery, completely
untamable and self-destructive. I think it is safe to say that
he was in major bondage. Yet even with a legion of demons
controlling every thought and action, they could not keep
the man from running to Jesus' feet to worship. Think about
this. *Satan cannot keep you from Jesus.* If he had the authority to stop anyone, it would have been this man, but he
couldn't. He has no power to keep you from the One who
died to save you and set you free.

Again, Jesus is not impressed with Satan and his minions.
They have to beg Him for mercy to suffer even such a fate as
indwelling a herd of suicidal pigs! Jesus has ultimate authority and power. No matter how much bondage you are in, no

matter how long you have been there, Jesus can set you free. He is that big. He is that powerful. He is that loving.

Hereditary sin, unforgiveness, traumatic memories, occultist practices and habitual sin—every time, these shortcomings open gates to let the thief in. No doubt, every one of us has had some level of experience with each of them. Whether or not you are a Christian is not the issue here because even believers can be in bondage. I just ask you, as you examine your past, your heart and your current spiritual condition, where is the enemy holding you prisoner? What is your bondage?

I want to lead you in a prayer to help you turn to Jesus with honest confession and utter dependence upon His power for deliverance. As you read, pray from your heart these sincere words that block those gates Satan has been using to sneak into your life:

*Lord, I come to You with open hands, not holding anything back from You. In Jesus' name, I come to confess my own wickedness and the iniquities of my fathers. Apply the blood of Jesus and forgive the sins we have committed against You. By Your mercy, cut off any continuing iniquity that is cursing our family. Set us free from that bondage.*

*Lord, You know the unforgiveness I've harbored in my heart. Today, I let go of it. I release every person from every hurt they have ever caused me. In Jesus' name, forgive me and set me free from the tormenters who have harassed me for so long.*

*As for my memories of trauma, Lord, I ask for Your tender hand of healing. Replace any lie I have believed with Your truth. Help me to walk in Your love that casts out all of my fears. Push the enemy back, out of the control he has had over me since that time.*

*Lord, I ask Your forgiveness for any participation I have had in witchcraft and the occult. I renounce Satan and his kingdom. Give me wisdom, Father, to see and flee any activity of witchcraft. Help me not to exalt Satan but to glorify You in all that I do. Protect my family from the infiltration of the occult so we will not be bound on the enemy's territory.*

*Finally, Lord, You know my heart better than I do. You know which areas of sin I cling to, run to and habitually choose over You. Set me free from the power that sin holds over me so I can choose to serve You instead. I want You to lead me to the life of righteousness.*

*Thank You, God, for the freedom You provide. Help me to walk in it every day. Protect me from the evil one and give me victory over his schemes. I receive Your forgiveness and Your freedom in Jesus' name. Amen.*

CHAPTER THREE

# WILL THE REAL JESUS PLEASE STAND UP?

When my son's friend heard the title of this chapter, he asked if I copied it from an Eminem song, to which I sarcastically responded, "Son, the only M&M I know is a candy!"

Actually, I got the idea for this chapter from an old game show way before my son's time. It was called *To Tell the Truth*, and the premise was that three people claimed to be the same person. Each challenger tried to convince a panel of four celebrities that his or her story was true. The panel interrogated them and later voted on which challenger they believed to be telling the truth. To reveal the true identity at the end of the show, the host would ask, "Will the real (person's name) please stand up?"

In today's church, I feel like we are playing this game with the person of Christ. I've seen so many people convinced that Jesus is one way when the Bible clearly tells us He is another. In this chapter, I want to take us to Scripture so once and for all, the real Jesus can stand above the rest and the posers claiming to be Jesus will be forced to sit down:

> *3 But I fear, lest somehow, as the serpent deceived Eve by his craftiness, so your minds may be corrupted from the simplicity that is in Christ. 4 For if he who comes preaches another Jesus whom we have not preached, or if you receive a different spirit which you have not received, or a different gospel which you have not accepted—you may well put up with it!* (2 Corinthians 11:3–4)

My concern is that slowly, over time, Satan has deceived many into believing in a Jesus not of the Bible. The enemy doesn't care if you believe in Jesus as long as it is the wrong Jesus. When you believe in the wrong Jesus, Satan knows you will never be free from bondage. Faith in a false version of Jesus means you miss out on knowing God and all Jesus came to accomplish on your behalf.

The most common false Jesus I see preached today is a Jesus who came to save people and get them to heaven but is incapable of helping them here on earth. Those who follow this Jesus are left alone to fight for their marriages, fend off sickness or overcome financial hardship. Churches who proclaim this Jesus teach that the Jesus of the Bible only did miracles to prove that He was God, and once He proved

Himself, He stopped acting supernaturally in people's lives. Basically, Jesus can get you to heaven, but it will be hell on earth until you get there!

I'm not trying to put down churches, but I do want to shed some light on one of Satan's schemes. He has been deceiving the church for nearly 2,000 years, and we need to be on guard to the way he is tricking us.

When Jesus started His ministry at age 30, He began by proclaiming the kingdom of heaven was at hand, healing the sick and casting out demons everywhere He went. People were intrigued by His teaching and impressed by His miracles. All over, people were curious about this man who spoke and acted with such authority. Then Jesus went back to His hometown.

In Nazareth, Jesus was not known as a prophet, teacher or healer. He was a carpenter, just like His dad. No doubt word had traveled and some in Nazareth had heard what Jesus had been up to, but to them, Jesus was just a carpenter. So when He came into town and went to the synagogue to speak, his neighbors obliged. None expected much from Him, but what came out of His mouth shocked and horrified them:

> *16 So He came to Nazareth, where He had been brought up. And as His custom was, He went into the synagogue on the Sabbath day, and stood up to read. 17*

*And He was handed the book of the prophet Isaiah. And when He had opened the book, He found the place where it was written:*

*[18] "The Spirit of the Lord is upon Me, Because He has anointed Me To preach the gospel to the poor; He has sent Me to heal the brokenhearted, To proclaim liberty to the captives And recovery of sight to the blind, To set at liberty those who are oppressed; [19] To proclaim the acceptable year of the Lord."*

*[20] Then He closed the book, and gave it back to the attendant and sat down. And the eyes of all who were in the synagogue were fixed on Him. [21] And He began to say to them, "Today this Scripture is fulfilled in your hearing"* (Luke 4:16–21).

Right there, Jesus made the most amazing, controversial statement He could have made in His hometown. Basically, He picked up an old prophecy (from Isaiah 61), one that all of Israel had been waiting to be fulfilled for hundreds of years, one pointing to the ultimate Messiah of God. Jesus claimed to be that man. In that moment in the synagogue at Nazareth, Jesus stood up and said, "This is the real me."

As you can imagine, that didn't go over well. That would be like your neighbor knocking on your door and announcing himself to be the president of the United States. You wouldn't take him very seriously. The townspeople in Nazareth didn't just blow Jesus off; they knew what that prophecy meant. They knew that Isaiah was speaking of their long-awaited Messiah, and they became enraged that Jesus would claim such greatness when He was obviously just a carpenter.

> So all those in the synagogue, when they heard these things, were filled with wrath, [29] and rose up and thrust Him out of the city; and they led Him to the brow of the hill on which their city was built, that they might throw Him down over the cliff (Luke 4:28–29).

Jesus preached His first sermon in His hometown, and they tried to kill Him—all because He told them He was more than a carpenter. He was the Messiah, the one they had been waiting on to usher in the acceptable year of the Lord. Today, we may not want to throw Jesus off a cliff, but so many who claim to be His followers do not believe Jesus is all He claimed to be in this passage. Out of the Isaiah prophecy, Jesus revealed five foundational ministries He came to accomplish: salvation, anointing, emotional healing, physical healing and deliverance.

If you are worshipping a Jesus who can only get you to heaven but can't help you out on earth, you've got the wrong Jesus! We must embrace Jesus for all He came to accomplish and allow Him to do these things in and through us in our lifetimes.

## JESUS CAME TO SAVE

Jesus' first ministry, the primary reason He came, was to save us and reunite us with God. This ministry is mentioned twice in the passage, at the beginning and at the end: *The Spirit of the LORD is upon me ... to preach the gospel to the poor ... to proclaim the acceptable year of the LORD* (Luke 4:18–19).

"Gospel" means good news. Jesus came to preach good news; He didn't come to share good advice or talk about good options. Essentially, the good news He came to proclaim is that you are a sinner, desperately in need of someone to rescue you, and I have come to do just that. Now you can be reconciled to God and be with Him forever. That, my friend, is good news ... the best news for everyone who hears and believes.

To add to that good news, Jesus came to *proclaim the acceptable year of the Lord,* which means now is the time that salvation is available. Before Jesus came, man couldn't accept God or be accepted by God. Sin stood in the way. In Jesus, you can accept God and God can accept you.

If you haven't encountered Jesus on this first and most important level, then let me encourage you: repent and believe. The Bible says that you have sinned against God and are personally responsible for that sin. Turn from your sin and put your faith in Jesus, whose death and resurrection was on your behalf so He could forgive you and make you right with God. No one else can do that for you; you have to have the faith. It doesn't matter if you were baptized as a baby or if your parents were Christians. You are accountable for the state of your heart, whether you walk apart from God or by faith in Jesus Christ.

Also, it is vital that you make public your decision to accept Jesus as your Savior. Jesus Himself said, *Therefore whoever confesses Me before men, him I will also confess before My Father who is in heaven. But whoever denies Me before men, him I will also deny before My Father who is in heaven* (Matthew 10:32). In Romans, Paul explains *that if you confess with your mouth the Lord Jesus and believe in your heart that God has raised Him from the dead, you will be saved. For with the heart one believes unto righteousness, and with the mouth confession is made unto salvation* (Romans 10:9–10).

Jesus' first and primary ministry is to save, and we should never diminish how He accomplished salvation for us. We should also never forget that His work on the cross accomplished so much more than just getting us to heaven. The salvation He offers has more far-reaching effects.

## JESUS CAME TO ANOINT

At Jesus' baptism, the Holy Spirit descended upon Him. Then, before His ministry began, He spent 40 days in the wilderness, fasting and praying. When He came out of the desert, the Bible says He was filled with the power of the Holy Spirit to start preaching, healing and casting out demons. If Jesus, being God in the flesh, needed the anointing of the Holy Spirit when He walked this earth, how much more do you and I need that anointing as well?

When we place our faith in Jesus, at that moment, the Holy Spirit baptizes us into the Body of Christ (1 Corinthians 12:13). But the Bible tells us that Jesus wants to baptize us with the Holy Spirit (Matthew 3:11; Mark 1:8; Luke 3:16; John 1:33). Jesus explicitly told His disciples to wait for the baptism in the Holy Spirit (Acts 1:4–8; Luke 24:49). Each of us needs this anointing from on high, and this is specifically one of the ministries of Jesus.

At our church, Gateway Church, we offer Freedom Ministry where we walk people through these five ministries of Jesus. We try to communicate all Jesus came to give His followers, including the filling of the Holy Spirit, so those who come to us can walk in the fullness and abundance of their salvation.

When we were a very small church meeting in a day-care building, Chad Hennings (a three-time Super Bowl champion for the Dallas Cowboys) and his family started coming. Chad became a Christian, and when I baptized him, I had to sort of fold him down to get all six feet six inches into the baptistery. As Chad grew in the Lord, his desire to receive the fullness of Jesus' life grew as well. When he heard about all that Jesus came to offer him, Chad came to Pastor Brady Boyd and me to help him understand and take hold of all Jesus has to offer.

Pastor Brady and I started praying for Chad, and the Holy Spirit was noticeably present. Chad was particularly overcome and began to feel lightheaded. Now, before I go on, I want to clarify that I never, ever push people down when I am praying for them. Most of the time, if they start to fall, I hold them because I am not done praying for them yet. When Chad started rocking, I wasn't finished praying. With my one hand on his chest and the other on his back, I tried to hold him up, but Chad is a 280-pound defensive lineman ... you can see where this is heading.

Becoming increasingly unsteady, Chad started to fall forward ... right where Pastor Brady was standing. I opened my eyes just in time to see the expression of panic on Pastor Brady's face. Between the two of us, we managed to steer his timber toward the couch where he lay for another five minutes or so under the power of God. Right there in our office, Chad experienced the anointing ministry of Jesus for the first time in his life.

Friends, it is a good thing to be filled with the presence

of God over and over again. As you yield to the Holy Spirit, He will fill you so your daily journey is empowered by His love, His grace, His kindness and His ability. He can flow through you to help you be a better husband, wife, father, mother, friend, employee, neighbor or whatever.

Jesus didn't just come to give you a better life in heaven. He came to give you a better life on earth by the anointing and filling of His Spirit. You don't have to struggle along in your own strength day after day, failing over and over, never able to get it right. The very strength of God is available to you as a free and amazing gift you simply have to receive. Jesus already has done what it takes for us to walk in the power of the Spirit, so all we have to do is receive the baptism in the Holy Spirit and welcome Him into our lives every day.

Don't settle for a powerless, defeated life. Jesus was anointed by the Holy Spirit, and now He offers the same anointing to you. Ask Him for it and walk in God's presence daily. You will be amazed at the difference it makes in every aspect of life.

## JESUS CAME TO HEAL YOUR HEART

Has someone ever disappointed you so deeply that it broke your heart? When disappointment settles in, Satan is there to take advantage of your low point and hold you in bondage to that pain. He deceives us into thinking he can deliver comfort when all he can really deliver is more sorrow.

The Bible warns us of how the devil manages to hold so many of us in bondage. *And no wonder! For Satan himself transforms himself into an angel of light. Therefore it is no great thing if his ministers also transform themselves into ministers of righteousness, whose end will be according to their works* (2 Corinthians 11:14–15). Satan is a pretender, and he shows up in your darkest moments disguised as light. Then he lures you into his darkness and holds you prisoner.

Let's say you find out that your good friend spread some slanderous remarks about you. Your feelings are deeply hurt, and immediately one of the devil's helpers is at your side, whispering in your ear, "How dare she say that after all you've done for her. And all those people listened to her! Your name is ruined." It feels so good right away to revel in your anger and feel justified in your pain. That is how a demon, a minister of darkness, can pass himself off to you as an angel of light. But don't be deceived.

No matter how comforting those whispers sound, they will only lead you to traps of bitterness. The enemy is planting unforgiveness and distrust in your heart, so instead of forgiving and loving your sister, you push her away, hold her at a distance and are tortured in your own heart for the darkness you have let in.

Men, maybe an example in your life has to do with a brother or father who put you down as a child. His harsh words may still ring in your ears today, and all along, the devil has been there pouring salt into your open wound: "You'll never have enough or be enough to impress him. Why try?" It may seem comforting to have a spirit agreeing with your pain and offering you an excuse not to become who God created you to be, but Satan's lies only keep you in bondage to that pain.

Feelings are strong, but the truth is stronger. Despite what you may think, you can control how you feel because your feelings will follow suit with your actions. When you choose to ignore the enemy's whisper in your ear and obey God's Word in the midst of your pain, you will be amazed how your emotions fall in line. You may not want to forgive, but unforgiveness is only delivering you over to torturers. As hard as it may be to forgive, as much as you don't think you could ever *feel* like you've forgiven the person who hurt you, the healing that comes with forgiveness is worth your obedience.

A lifetime of disappointment and pain has left us all in need of a healer. Our hearts are broken and scarred from years of mistreatment. They are mangled and marred to the point that we think them unhealable, but Jesus said in Luke 4:18 *He has sent Me to heal the brokenhearted ... To set at liberty those who are oppressed.* That word for "oppressed" means bruised. The bruising of your heart holds you captive, but Jesus came to heal your soul and set you free from that bondage.

When I was a little boy, I had to go to a speech therapist because I could not correctly pronounce the letter "R." For some children who struggle with this, it is not a traumatic problem, but for me it was. Had my name been Tom Lane, maybe I would have coped better, but every time someone asked me my name, I responded, "Wobewt Mowwis." It was humiliating.

Decades later, I was going through a time of inner healing, and the man who was praying for me told me to ask God to bring memories to mind that He wanted to heal for me. As memories came up, my friend counseled me to submit them to the Lord, and I did as he instructed. Memories started to come, and though they were stressful at first, I submitted them to the Lord, who took the stress away. God was touching me, healing me of wounds I had long learned to live with.

Then the Lord gave my friend a word of knowledge to speak over me. He said he saw a little boy on the playground hiding from the other kids because he couldn't pronounce his Rs. Instantly, like a flood, it all came back to me. Memories flooded my mind, and the wound was as fresh as that day on the playground. The spirits of fear and rejection that had taken advantage of me as a child flew back in my face. I had suppressed that memory so far down because it hurt so much, but God wanted to bring it up again in order to heal me. And He did. He healed me of that wound.

If you have painful memories, and I know you do because we all do, God wants to set you free from the pain, shame or hurt they have caused for so many years. In His presence is the safest place to be when you revisit those times. He is gentle, loving, compassionate and has the power to make those open, bloody wounds like baby flesh once again. He can restore you. He can heal you. He can set you free.

## JESUS CAME TO HEAL YOUR BODY

Luke 4:18 goes on to say, *And recovery of sight to the blind.* This refers to physical healing. Look what happens later on in this same chapter:

> *38 Now [Jesus] arose from the synagogue and entered Simon's house. But Simon's wife's mother was sick with a high fever, and they made request of Him concerning her. 39 So He stood over her and rebuked the fever, and it left her. And immediately she arose and served them.*
>
> *40 When the sun was setting, all those who had any that were sick with various diseases brought them to Him; and He laid His hands on every one of them and healed them* (Luke 4:38–40).

The real Jesus is a natural and generous healer. It flows

from Him, and it's as if He can't help but minister to the sick and needy around Him. When He came to Simon's mother, He didn't stand over her and offer to *only* get her to heaven. He didn't turn His face from her need ... He healed her. As the crowds came with sicknesses, He didn't pick and choose whom He healed ... He healed them all!

If you serve a Jesus who doesn't heal, you serve the wrong Jesus. Jesus still heals today. I know this because the Bible tells me that Jesus doesn't change. His character *is the same yesterday, today and forever* (Hebrews 13:8). If God is perfect at this moment, He cannot change. Improvement would imply He is not currently perfect, and a change for the worse would obviously negate His perfect status. God can't change because He is holy and perfect just as He is today and has always been.

Jesus is God, so if God doesn't change, Jesus doesn't change. His character is the same today as when He walked on earth. So if Jesus healed when He walked on earth, He still heals today. Healing is not only what He does, it is who He is. The real Jesus, the Jesus of the Bible, is so full of compassion and power that His nature is to help and heal the physically broken.

When Jesus sent out His followers, He gave them instructions to do three things: preach the gospel of the kingdom, heal the sick and cast out demons. This was the first time in His ministry that He called others to join Him in His work, and these are the three things He told them to do. We've already talked about the priority of the gospel message to save people—the first reason Jesus came. But He also told them to heal and cast out demons. To Jesus, these ministries were also important.

If healing was that important to Jesus, it should be just as important to us.

I know that people or churches misapply the truth of Jesus' power to heal. Don't fall into their traps and get into more bondage over them. Pray for healing. Believe in Jesus' power to heal, but if He doesn't heal you right away, don't let anyone tell you that it is your fault. There is no condemnation in the area of healing. It is not always about how much faith you have or how much sin you have. You can't conjure up Jesus' power to heal you by believing more or sinning less. Healing is all about Jesus showing up in compassion to deliver you from a physical ailment. Ask Him to. Expect Him to. But don't beat yourself up while you wait for Him to answer.

Embracing the real Jesus means believing His power is still present today to set people free from physical bondage. If you grew up in a church that taught healing was just for Jesus' time and not for today, this may be hard to accept. If you will look at Jesus' ministry and see His compassion for the sick and lame, you will discover the Jesus of the Bible. That is the real Jesus. How awesome that we don't serve a Jesus unable or unwilling to meet us in our immediate need of pain. He is big enough and good enough to heal us and set us free.

## JESUS CAME TO DELIVER

Some people in Jesus' day were set in their idea of who God was and what He could do. They didn't like Jesus challenging their orthodoxy and took every opportunity to try to prove His teaching and His miracles to be false. Consider this account from Luke, when Jesus cast out a demon, restoring the life of a mute man:

> *14 And He was casting out a demon, and it was mute. So it was, when the demon had gone out, that the mute spoke; and the multitudes marveled. 15 But some of them said, "He casts out demons by Beelzebub, the ruler of the demons"* (Luke 11:14–15).

Now tell me, does it even make sense that Satan would cast himself out? Isn't that self-defeating? Some people will think of any excuse not to believe that Jesus is who He said He is and to discredit the fact that the miracles He performed were by the power of God. Look at this next verse. It's just as amazing. *Others, testing Him, sought from Him a sign from heaven* (Luke 11:16).

A sign from heaven? What miracle did these people

just witness? The text says Jesus cast out a demon that had caused a man to be mute; the evidence that Jesus actually did cast out the demon was that the mute spoke. How did they miss this *sign from heaven?*

Jesus responded to the people's doubts:

> *[17] But He, knowing their thoughts, said to them: "Every kingdom divided against itself is brought to desolation, and a house divided against a house falls. [18] If Satan also is divided against himself, how will his kingdom stand? Because you say I cast out demons by Beelzebub. [19] And if I cast out demons by Beelzebub, by whom do your sons cast them out? Therefore they will be your judges. [20] But if I cast out demons with the finger of God, surely the kingdom of God has come upon you"* (Luke 11:17–20).

Jesus can be downright funny sometimes. He said to them, "Okay, if you think I'm casting these demons out by Beelzebub and are so unhappy about that, how exactly are you getting them out?" No one answered because everyone knew ... they weren't getting them out! Without Jesus, people were destined to suffer for life with the torment and possession of evil spirits. The good news, whether some people there wanted to accept it or not, was that the very kingdom of God had come into their presence because Jesus had cast out darkness right in their midst.

To explain Himself, Jesus continued with a parable:

> [21] *When a strong man, fully armed, guards his own palace, his goods are in peace.* [22] *But when a stronger than he comes upon him and overcomes him, he takes from him all his armor in which he trusted, and divides his spoils.* [23] *He who is not with Me is against Me, and he who does not gather with Me scatters"* (Luke 11:21–23).

I've heard some misinterpret this parable by saying that you and I are the strong man, and we must guard our houses so the devil doesn't come along and take over. This is not what Jesus is saying. Jesus' message is much more powerful than that. No man is strong enough to withstand the devil alone, so we can't be the strong man in the parable. Jesus was actually referring to the mute man He had just delivered from an evil spirit. Satan had that man in bondage for years; he was the strong man, fully armed and guarding his palace. The devil thought he was secure, but Jesus, the stronger one, came along and overcame. The parable was like a prophecy about the future of the enemy who believes himself safe and strong; in the end, Jesus will take everything he has.

To those doubters in the crowd, Jesus was saying, "Right in front of your eyes stands the One who is more powerful than the enemy who has held you in bondage your whole life. I am stronger than the devil, and I can set you free!"

Friends, *He who is in you is greater than he who is in the world* (1 John 4:4). You don't have to fear the devil as long as you fear and honor God—He is your protection and deliverance. It doesn't matter if your family doubts. It doesn't matter if people at your church are suspicious of asking Jesus to do anything as supernatural as to set you free from the bondage of the evil one. This is your chance to embrace the real Jesus and tap into all the power He came to spend on your behalf.

So I ask you: what Jesus do you serve? Does He save? Does He anoint with His Spirit? Does He heal hearts? Does He heal bodies? Does He set people free from the grip of darkness? If not, you aren't serving the real Jesus. I pray that what you have read in this chapter has allowed you to see the real Jesus standing a head above the other posers. I pray too that you would put all your faith and hope in that Jesus, and in that Jesus alone.

It is my passion to hold up the real Jesus for all to see. I don't want anyone to settle for less than the Jesus portrayed in Matthew, Mark, Luke and John. I've seen the devastating effects of those who receive a Jesus who can get them to heaven but reject the other four reasons He came. In fact, I've grieved over loved ones in my own family who never embraced the full reality of Jesus.

My grandfather did not know the Lord when he was raising his family. When my father was 16, a Christian man came into my grandfather's life and invited him to his home so he could share the gospel. That night, my grandfather let my dad drive him to the man's house but told my dad to wait on the porch while he went in to hear what the man had to say. On the porch of that neighbor's house, listening through the screen door, my father heard the gospel for the first time in his life. My grandfather did not believe that day, but my dad did.

My dad had two younger brothers. All three of them went to churches that taught them that Jesus could get them to heaven but couldn't really do anything else to help them in this life. The elder of my father's brothers became an alcoholic and led a destructive life. When his addiction threatened to ruin his family, he went to the church for help and the church sent him to AA. I have nothing against AA, but what my uncle needed was Jesus, the real Jesus who has the power to deliver and heal.

As my uncle got older, my father and I told him over and over again that God could help him, but he just couldn't believe it. He only knew the Jesus who gave tickets to heaven. In his mind, a Jesus who could set him free from alcoholism just didn't exist. In his late 60s, he was imprisoned, and I watched my dad cry over the possibility that his brother would die there never having experienced the freedom and abundance of walking with God.

My other uncle walked for years without Jesus at all. He was divorced three times and married four. He served in Vietnam as a door gunner where his job was to kill those who posed a threat, including children whom the enemy sent out with grenades strapped to them. Once, he shot a child whom he thought had a bomb, but then realized the child was only carrying a toy truck. When he returned from his duty, he was completely messed up and demonized, waking up in the middle of the night with the most tormenting nightmares.

After a while, he went to a church that preached a Jesus who could forgive and save him. He accepted that salvation and started doing better. He married his original wife, and his life seemed to be getting back on track. They kept attending the church, but my uncle never learned what Jesus could do about the suffering in his soul left over from the trauma of war. He begged for help with his emotional struggles, but the church had nothing to offer. After two years, he put a gun to his head and killed himself because he couldn't escape the memories and demons taunting him day and night.

The topic of discovering and knowing the real Jesus is near to my heart because I have seen firsthand how an inadequate knowledge of Him is so destructive to the life of a believer. Jesus came to give His people breakthroughs in every area of bondage they suffer—spiritual, emotional and physical. A church may have told you that you just have to suffer with the pain, the memories, the demons or whatever is holding you back. Satan may have convinced you that you can never be free. But he is wrong. Freedom is available to you. You don't have to live this way anymore.

Jesus, the real Jesus, stands ready to be anything and everything you need. His love is enough to set you free, and His power is enough to accomplish even the impossible.

CHAPTER FOUR

# BREAKTHROUGH OR BREAKDOWN

God did not create you to be a victim or a casualty. As God's child, you are not destined to be the enemy's prey, open and vulnerable to attack. *Freedom: Your Birthright as a Believer* is all about finally taking hold of the fullness of life Jesus died to give you. You were bought with a very high price, so you should be walking in victory and in the abundance of your potential.

Throughout the pages of the Old Testament, the lives of men and women are recounted for us to learn from and, in many cases, emulate. Some of them show us what happens when we don't follow God, and others show us what can happen when God's grace and favor rest soundly upon us. The first type always ended up breaking down in defeat, but the second, the ones who received God's guidance and followed His ways, always broke through to victory. There is perhaps no greater contrast between these two types of people than David and Saul.

Saul was the first appointed king of Israel. The Bible says he was a tall and handsome man, well loved and accepted by the people. God appointed him, and he started out leading God's people well. He became a fierce warrior, fighting and winning battles against great odds, until he entered into willful disobedience and rebellion against God's ways. God rejected Saul as king, causing Saul to enter into the long and painful decline of his reign.

David was the second king of Israel, and like Saul, he was appointed by God. Stories of David's bravery even as a boy are remarkable: he killed a lion and a bear in hand-to-paw combat. While he was still a very young man, and before he ever took the throne as the king of Israel, David accomplished what is known even today as one of the greatest feats of strength and courage—he conquered a giant.

In this last chapter, I want to walk you through this story and show you what it looks like to achieve great victory in the face of impossible odds. I also want to show you what it looks like to suffer great defeat, not to physical armies, but to the bondage of the enemy. The same enemy faced both men. David turned out to be a hero; Saul turned out to be a heartache.

## CONFIDENCE OR FEAR?

The story opens after Saul had already disobeyed God, and God rejected him as king. Through the prophet Samuel, God anointed David to become the next king, but it was many years before this exchange of power actually took place. But it only took God's rejection for Saul to sink into great depression.

> *14 But the Spirit of the Lord departed from Saul, and a distressing spirit from the Lord troubled him. 15 And Saul's servants said to him, "Surely, a distressing spirit from God is troubling you. 16 Let our master now command your servants, who are before you, to seek out a man who is a skillful player on the harp. And it shall be that he will play it with his hand when the distressing spirit from God is upon you, and you shall be well."*

> *17 So Saul said to his servants, "Provide me now a man who can play well, and bring him to me"* (1 Samuel 16:14–17).

There are no external remedies for depression or fear. Only God's Spirit can truly comfort and release you from such tormenting emotions, and only significant and eternal changes in your heart will give you lasting relief from such bondage. Calling on a harpist to sooth his soul, Saul was looking for a quick fix, a temporary solution. He was not seeking the healing balm of God for his wounded spirit, and without this, his anxiety, distress and fear would only carry on into even more difficult seasons of life.

You may have heard this story before and know the harpist Saul's servants found for him was young David. Saul did not know that David had been chosen to take his place as king. All Saul knew was what his servants had reported to him about David's reputation: *a son of Jesse the Bethlehemite, who is skillful in playing, a mighty man of valor, a man of war, prudent in speech, and a handsome person; and the Lord is with him* (I Samuel 16:18). So David came and played, and Saul was calmed for a season.

Then life got complicated. The Philistine army, Israel's archenemy, came against them with an interesting challenge for battle: their champion, Goliath, would take on Israel's champion in a one-on-one fight to the death and winner-take-all battle.

Saul and David had remarkably different responses to Goliath. Saul, along with the rest of his army, *were dismayed and greatly afraid* (I Samuel 17:11). I can't say I blame them exactly. Goliath, as you may have heard, was a giant over 9 feet tall. His armor of bronze weighed as much as a man. When he stood with his javelin and spear, taunting the army of Israel, I'm not sure I wouldn't have been a bit scared myself.

But Saul shouldn't have been so intimidated. He had fought many battles and overcome great odds before. If he were the same Saul God had appointed as king and if he had retained the Spirit of God with him, he would have taken his sword, walked straight out on that field and put an end to the battle once and for all.

But that is not what Saul, the king of Israel, did. *And all the men of Israel, [including Saul], when they saw [Goliath], fled from him and were dreadfully afraid* (1 Samuel 17:24). It was David, a shepherd boy, a harpist, who took courage and stepped up to the plate. When he looked at Goliath, he didn't see a giant too big to conquer. He saw an enemy of God defying God's people.

> *32 Then David said to Saul, "Let no man's heart fail because of him; your servant will go and fight with this Philistine."*

> *33 And Saul said to David, "You are not able to go against this Philistine to fight with him; for you are a youth, and he a man of war from his youth."*

> *34 But David said to Saul, "Your servant used to keep his father's sheep, and when a lion or a bear came and took a lamb out of the flock, 35 I went out after it and struck it, and delivered the lamb from its mouth;*

*and when it arose against me, I caught it by its beard, and struck and killed it. ³⁶ Your servant has killed both lion and bear; and this uncircumcised Philistine will be like one of them, seeing he has defied the armies of the living God." ³⁷ Moreover David said, "The Lord, who delivered me from the paw of the lion and from the paw of the bear, He will deliver me from the hand of this Philistine."*

*And Saul said to David, "Go, and the Lord be with you!"* (1 Samuel 17:32–37).

David was a man of courage. Saul was appointed the leader of Israel, but he abdicated his rights. He had lost his calling, his way in life, and with it, he lost the confidence he once had in God. Young David now had that confidence and stepped forward in boldness to be the man God would use to deliver His people from their enemies.

What has God called you to be or do? Have you lost your footing or your way? Is there an enemy staring you in the face, threatening to beat you and force you into bondage? The choice is clear: will you be confident, or will you be afraid? Will you run to the battle knowing that God will make you victorious, or will you flee in fear?

Satan is no respecter of persons either. He does not hold back his attacks just because you are a Christian. In fact, he is probably more likely to come after you because you are a threat to him! Jesus tells us that just as the sun rises on both good and bad people, rain falls on both (Matthew 5:45). You are not exempt from trials, battles, temptations or bondage, but you can be exempt from defeat.

Like David, you have the Spirit of God inside of you. The Spirit was the source of his confidence and can be the source of yours as well. How can a believer who has the Holy Spirit inside of him walk around in a spirit of fear or defeat? We should be the boldest, most confident, people on the planet because God abides in us!

One practical way you can stop cowering in fear and walk in the confidence of the Lord is to regularly speak your testimony. Look back at what God has already accomplished for you. David remembered how God strengthened him to kill a lion and a bear, and he recited the tales to Saul. What has God done for you? The act of raising you from death to life by the blood of His Son should be enough to give you all the confidence in the world.

Speak your testimony out loud as often as possible. The more you tell it to your children, your neighbors, your fellow believers, the more you will hear it, and the more it will encourage you continually to have confidence in God. The more you talk about God's goodness to take care of you, the more you will remind the enemy that God is fighting your battles for you. Revelation 12:11 says that

Satan is overcome by the blood of the Lamb and by the power of the saints' testimony.

Don't act like Saul who didn't trust God to give him victory. Stand up in the fullness of what you have in Christ. Remember how He has been faithful to you in the past and move forward in the power and triumph He died to make available to you.

## YOURSELF OR SOMEONE ELSE

David and Saul were very different people, especially at this particular moment in history. Their lives had looked very different up to this point. Saul was a king, had been in the heat of battle and had resources and skills David couldn't imagine. David was just a shepherd boy.

When David determined to fight Goliath, Saul presented him with the finest armor of the day—an offer that would tempt most warriors today.

> *[38] So Saul clothed David with his armor, and he put a bronze helmet on his head; he also clothed him with a coat of mail. [39] David fastened his sword to his armor and tried to walk, for he had not tested them. And David said to Saul, "I cannot walk with these, for I have not tested them." So David took them off* (1 Samuel 17:38–39).

Going into this battle, David knew he was not Saul, and he knew trying to be like Saul wouldn't bring him victory. God had delivered the lion and bear into his hands when he was unarmed and unprotected. That was how God had trained him to fight and that was the training he trusted.

*Then he took his staff in his hand; and he chose for himself five smooth stones from the brook, and put them in a shepherd's bag, in a pouch which he had, and his sling was in his hand. And he drew near to the Philistine (1 Samuel 17:40).*

Saul was probably one of David's boyhood heroes from stories of the mighty king conquering Israel's adversaries, but God had given David enough wisdom not to fall into the trap of envy. Had David compared himself to Saul, he never would have even offered to fight Goliath: "Saul has fought so many battles. He has so much more experience with this kind of thing. If he can't do this, how can I?" David didn't go there. He saw himself as God saw him, and he used what God had given him to accomplish the task God had put before him.

Had David walked into battle with Saul's armor, he could have died. He was not an expert swordsman. Later in life, he did become a mighty warrior skilled with the sword, but he was still a young man, inexperienced in battle. All he needed for this fight was a rock and a sling.

God has gifted each of His children with unique talents, skills, personalities and experiences. You were created for this time, this place in history to contribute what God has given you to the advancement of His kingdom. Whatever battles face you, these are the same tools you are to use for fighting the enemy. You were designed to be an overcomer, not by becoming like someone else, but by being who you are.

Some people in the church categorize the spiritual gifts, lifting some to a higher importance than others. God never did this. No matter what your gifts are, they are no less than anyone else's. If God has given you a sling and five rocks, use them with faith and confidence. Maybe one day He'll equip you with a sword, not because it is better, but because it is more suited to your need. Until then, use what you've been given to slay your Goliath.

You and I have a promise to claim from Scripture: ... *His divine power has given to us all things that pertain to life and godliness, through the knowledge of Him who called us by glory and virtue, by which have been given to us exceedingly great and precious promises, that through these you may be partakers of the divine nature* ... (2 Peter 1:3–4). We've got it all, everything we need to navigate these days of hardship, bondage and trial, and if you think someone else has what you need, you are wrong. God has given *you* exactly what *you* need, *everything* you need for life and godliness.

David didn't try to become or even compete with Saul. As the man God had created him to be, David walked onto the battlefield full of faith and confidence. In the face of the enemy, be yourself. Don't try to be someone you are not. Pull from the strengths and abilities God has given you and trust Him to be the power that will make you victorious.

## VICTOR OR VICTIM?

Are you ready to hear some serious Old Testament trash talkin'?

*42 And when the Philistine looked about and saw David, he disdained him; for he was only a youth, ruddy and good-looking. 43 So the Philistine said to David, "Am I a dog, that you come to me with sticks?" And the Philistine cursed David by his gods. 44 And the Philistine said to David, "Come to me, and I will give your flesh to the birds of the air and the beasts of the field!"*

*45 Then David said to the Philistine, "You come to me with a sword, with a spear, and with a javelin. But I come to you in the name of the Lord of hosts, the God of the armies of Israel, whom you have defied. 46 This day the Lord will deliver you into my hand, and I will strike you and take your head from you. And this day I will give the carcasses of the camp of the Philistines*

*to the birds of the air and the wild beasts of the earth,
that all the earth may know that there is a God in
Israel. ⁴⁷ Then all this assembly shall know that the
Lord does not save with sword and spear; for the battle
is the Lord's, and He will give you into our hands"*
(1 Samuel 17:42–47).

What did I tell you—trash talkin'. Goliath threatens, "Hey there little boy, I'm gonna feed you to the birds!" David retorts, "Oh yeah? God is on my side. I'm gonna chop your head off and turn you into animal chow." Goliath bragged on his own size, and David bragged on God's.

Winning doesn't take muscles or money. It doesn't take an army of people behind you. All it takes is the power of Jesus working in and through you. I know so many believers out there fighting battles, struggling to win, but there is no power behind them. Either they fight a battle they shouldn't be fighting at all, or they fight one God wants to fight on their behalf, but they aren't letting Him do it. What about you? Are you beat down by the battle? Are you tired, stressed, worried, afraid and doubtful? If so, you are not fighting like David ... you are fighting like Saul.

David went out confident as himself, and in the strength of the Lord, he experienced victory! He didn't regret his approach, and he didn't have to eat the words he flung at Goliath on the battlefield.

*48 So it was, when the Philistine arose and came and drew near to meet David, that David hurried and ran toward the army to meet the Philistine. 49 Then David put his hand in his bag and took out a stone; and he slung it and struck the Philistine in his forehead, so that the stone sank into his forehead, and he fell on his face to the earth. 50 So David prevailed over the Philistine with a sling and a stone, and struck the Philistine and killed him. But there was no sword in the hand of David. 51 Therefore David ran and stood over the Philistine, took his sword and drew it out of its sheath and killed him, and cut off his head with it* (1 Samuel 17:48–51).

This was hardly even a battle. They ran at each other, one stone flew through the air, and it was over. David beat Goliath. A shepherd boy conquered a giant. A harpist defeated a warrior. It wasn't by coincidence or luck. David wasn't hunkered behind a rock blindly lobbing stones, hoping against hope that God would come through. No, he ran hard into the battle using the strength, resources and ability God had given him, and these were enough ... enough to secure victory.

*This day* was the day of David's victory, and he fought with the confidence and valor of a man convinced that triumph was just a stone's throw away. Is that how you see the bondage and battles in your life? God has guaranteed victory to all His people, and His Spirit is not slow in supplying the power we need to see that victory come to pass.

Strange as it sounds, victory does come through surrender ... not surrender to your enemy but surrender to God. You have to completely depend on Him to come through for you. Victory was not in David's strength or good aim but in God applying His power through those things. Left alone, David would have suffered the very fate Goliath threatened—bird food—but backed by God, no giant was too big to take on.

Every day, we need God backing us as we face difficult decisions, enemies, temptations and all sorts of evil waiting to take us captive. We need God's strength, wisdom, favor and blessing to victoriously accomplish all that comes our way. James 4:10 says that if we humble ourselves before God, He will lift us up. This proves it is not your natural strength or ability that leads us to victory; it is God's power to work in and through you.

You may feel like the "strengths" God has given you are actually weaknesses. You look at your five tiny pebbles and your little, old sling and think, "I know God is supposed to have given me what I need, but these just won't do. They aren't enough." This statement is, in a way, both true and false.

It is true in the sense that no human ability is enough

to win battles against the strong enemies we are up against. The reality is that one stone put up against an armor of bronze is a pretty shabby match-up. But it is not true that the potential of success rests solely on what your rocks and sling can accomplish on their own. The Lord has said, *My grace is sufficient for you, for My strength is made perfect in weakness* (2 Corinthians 12:9). Even when your ability is weak, you still have the strength you need because God fills in the gaps with His own power.

That is why you never have to fear opposition no matter how strong or weak you feel. In the end, you aren't the one who will win the battle; God is. Your part now is to surrender your pride or doubt or whatever it is that is holding you back from fully trusting God to fight on your behalf. Once that is laid down, you are ready to run into the battle in the strength of the Lord, armed with whatever weapon He's provided and confident that once you meet your enemy, the victory will already be yours.

In the Garden of Eden, Adam and Eve walked with God in complete health, peace and abundance. That is the life God wants for all of His children. The enemy has waged war against God and God's people and does all he can to keep us from the fullness available to us through Christ. Goliath comes against us every day and claims he is bigger and stronger with the ability to crush us at will. But we are like David, backed by the most powerful being in the universe, empowered to accomplish greater feats than this world would believe.

> *And when the Philistines saw that their champion was dead, they fled* (1 Samuel 17:51).

That is the end of this story—victory. Not just David's victory over Goliath, but the army of Israel over the army of Philistia. This victory was ultimately God's over Satan. David and Goliath are a picture of what Jesus accomplished at the cross. Two thousand years ago, Jesus crushed Satan's head and defeated every demonic spirit in Satan's army. The battle is over, and the victory is secure.

Jesus saw Satan fall from heaven like lightning. God didn't just drop him out of heaven, He propelled that angel of darkness so furiously from His presence that it lit up the sky like lightning. Every time you face the enemy, every time he comes against your family, remind him of that nasty fall from glory he took so long ago. Remind him that Jesus has conquered hell and the grave. Remind him of the power and person you stand in. I promise you, Satan will flee.

When Satan looks at you, he does not see a weak child armed with a rock and a sling. He sees the resurrected Christ standing on your behalf. He may try to bluff and act like you're not a threat, but when you stand behind the power of Jesus, you will win. *"Not by might nor by power, but by My Spirit," says the LORD of hosts* (Zechariah 4:6).

My friend, a breakthrough in freedom is possible for you. In God's sovereignty, He destined you to walk in the heights of freedom. No Goliath can keep you from that if you will just take hold of the breakthrough secured for you in Christ. Turn and face your demons. Don't hide from them or cower in their presence. They hold nothing over you!

Run to the battle with confidence—100 percent of you knowing that 100 percent of God is with you—and the victory will be yours. This is your doorway out of a place of cowardice, fear, bondage or victimization. *Today* is the day of your breakthrough. Freedom is just a stone's throw away, so leave that bondage behind, run to the battle and finally break through to full, joyous and victorious freedom.

Freedom belongs to you. It's your birthright.

# NOTES

# NOTES

# NOTES

# NOTES

# NOTES